Youth *Alpha*

Leaders Manual

First published 1996
Reprinted 1996
Reprint 2 March 1997

Published by HTB Publications, Holy Trinity Brompton, Brompton Road, London SW7 1JA

Illustrations by Charlie Mackesy

Printed in the UK by TPS Print, 6 Warren Lane, London SE18 6BW
Telephone: 0181 317 2997

CONTENTS

YOUTH ALPHA AND HOW TO DO IT

This manual is an *Alpha* resource. The *Alpha* course is a practical introduction to the Christian faith. It was initiated by Holy Trinity Brompton in London and is now being run by thousands of churches throughout the UK, as well as overseas.

Today there is a desperate need within the Church to reach and keep young people. By the age of sixteen, it is estimated that 98% of young people who once attended church no longer do so. Recent statistics suggest that only 7% of those under 18 years of age have any regular contact with "organised religion".

Youth *Alpha* offers a fresh and creative approach to reaching young people with the good news of Jesus Christ.

This leaders' manual is an attempt to equip you to bring alive the truth of God's word to those who have grown tired of listening to it *and* those who have never heard it before.

It is not intended as a mandatory blueprint. Please ignore it if you have a successful course running already. This is meant as a resource to help and encourage you; it is not meant to stifle your own creativity.

Young people today

There is a tendency to view change negatively. As the teenage years involve quite dramatic and comprehensive change, the assumption is automatically made that the teenage years are a total "nightmare" for all concerned.

However, when given the time, space and freedom to express themselves, young people are often able to show incredible insight and sensitivity. They are full of great enthusiasm, boundless creativity and deep compassion. They can be wonderfully resourceful, honest and open.

Teenagers experience enormous changes as they develop from children into adults. Sometimes they act like an adult trapped in a child's body, sometimes like a child trapped inside an adult's body. They may appear very mature at times but their maturity is likely to be erratic. At other times they may appear very young but that does not necessarily mean that they are stupid.

Intellectual development. Young people move from a "concrete" way of thinking towards an ability to think in abstract ways.

Those from a non Christian or unchurched background tend to formulate a personally-tailored religion for themselves.

Concepts like sin, salvation and grace are taught on Youth *Alpha* in a style requiring the ability to think in the abstract.

Emotional and social development. Young people are searching for identity (trying to discover who they are and what they can do). This search for identity involves experimentation (new behaviour, new role models etc.). They sometimes experience big swings in their mood and temperament.

An increasing number come from divorced or dysfunctional homes. They find it hard to empathise with other people. They are more computer literate and less inclined to read books than a generation ago.

Young people today are media-wise and can be quite cynical (they have watched a quarter of a million adverts before they are twenty-five).

Spiritual development. Those brought up and nurtured in the Christian faith will reassess and perhaps abandon old interpretations of Christian teaching for a more mature way of thinking.

We can help their thought processes to mature by encouraging them to decide what is true for them personally as well as what they believe to be true about God.

They tend to suspect anyone's claim to truth. They may see objective truth as either authoritarian or impossible. Nearly every survey shows that while this new generation of young people has rejected established religion, they are nevertheless desperately hungry for spiritual reality.

THE YOUTH ALPHA LEADER

There is a well-worn cliché which states that "Christianity is caught, not taught". Youth *Alpha* represents a wonderful opportunity to model the Christian life to young people. A young person is much more likely to opt for the Youth *Alpha* course on the basis of their relationship with the leader rather than the content of the course itself. Our whole approach and attitude must show that we are totally committed to them (Philippians 2:5-8). In a few years time they may have forgotten most of the actual course, but they will all remember something about you. (How much of the history that you were taught in school can you remember now? I bet you remember your history teacher!)

The word became flesh and lived among us (John 1:14). We need to "live" among the young people. We must be prepared to go to their world and meet them on their terms.

They would rather that you were honest and open with them than that you were a brilliant leader who ran spectacularly successful Youth *Alpha* sessions. (Though of course it is possible to be both.)

It is people not programmes that count.

Young people may not read the Bible too often but when they spend time with you they will certainly "read" your life (see 1Thessalonians 2:8). If your relationship with Jesus is alive and kicking, you are bound to have an effect on them. You may never know what a positive effect you will have.

Find out as much as you can about them. What influences the young people you are in contact with? What is their culture like? What was the last film they saw? What is their favourite music? What "soaps" do they watch? What do they spend their money on?

Young people need to know that you love and accept them, unconditionally. They need to know that you are committed to spending time and energy with them without also demanding that they respond to your message, change and grow. This is a freeing kind of love which releases the young people from the tyranny of feeling that they have to please you.

Are you prepared to run a whole Youth *Alpha* course and see no "results" at the end of it?

> Young people don't care how much you
> know until they know how much you care.

They are not just fodder for the Youth *Alpha* course. Do not run the course because you feel "someone's got to". The young people will soon pick up on it. It would be better not to run the course at all.

Helping young people to grasp the good news of Christ through Youth *Alpha* is tremendously exciting. It is also a sacrifice. It will involve a commitment to pray and as well as a lot of time and bags of energy.

Ask God to show you his love and concern for them. Look forward to meeting with them. Tell them whenever you can how much you appreciate them for who they *are* and not just for what they *do*.

DON'T:

♦ Be too quick to judge outward appearances or appear too shocked by what they may tell you.

♦ Take a swing in mood or temperament too personally.

♦ Expect them to believe or do something you yourself would not be prepared to believe or do.

♦ Expect to get on brilliantly with every young person.

♦ Feel that every session or chat with a young person has to be what *you* call productive.

♦ Ever put them down or attack their self respect.

DO:

♦ Get involved with them. "Walk in their shoes".

♦ Be prepared to be vulnerable and open.

♦ Be prepared to listen to them.

♦ Be prepared to be confidential and trustworthy.

♦ Affirm and encourage them whenever you can.

♦ Be aware that physical contact can be open to misunderstanding.

♦ Pray for them.

♦ Enjoy yourself!

WHERE DO I START?

Youth *Alpha* is a means to an end, not an end in itself. Before setting up a Youth *Alpha* course it is worth considering some key questions:

♦ Are we prepared to commit ourselves to young people before, during and *after* the course has finished?

♦ Have we considered the implications (e.g. on time, family, social life) of taking on and running Youth *Alpha?*

♦ How do we plan to accommodate those young people who become Christians during the course?

♦ What about those who have not yet decided to follow Christ but are still seriously interested?

♦ What about those who attended the course but who appeared to show no interest at all?

♦ To what extent are parents, schools and the local church behind Youth *Alpha?*

♦ Who is praying for us and for the young people involved?

♦ To what extent is the local church prepared to change and adapt as a result of the Youth *Alpha* course?

Church youth group

Establish clear aims for the course. Youth *Alpha* is not just about getting people to a course, it is ultimately about presenting them with the truth of the Christian faith and then discipling them in that faith.

Ask God to highlight key young people. Some young people have enormous influence on their friends.

Establish a core group. (Be careful not to alienate anyone who genuinely wants to be involved.) Get them excited about Youth *Alpha*. Get their ideas and comments. Incorporate as many as possible into the course. The more your core group feel they own the Youth *Alpha* course the more likely they are to invite their friends.

Outside the local church youth group

Provide a service or activity where young people can wander in, have fun and get to know Christians. e.g. A coffee bar (make sure it has "cred") or night-club run by Christians. Organise football, softball, basketball, table-tennis. Get young people to invite their friends along, encourage a number of Christians to take part.

Build relationships. Encourage Christian young people to mix with those who are not Christians. Blade with the rollerbladers, hang out with those that hang out, pump iron with those that pump iron, devour "Big Macs" with those who do likewise...

Offer invitations to Youth *Alpha*. Have an eye catching leaflet which Christians can give to their friends.

Christian young people will only invite their friends if they have confidence in the material you are hoping to present.

Can you guarantee it is going to be "cringe-free" and "cred"?

It may help to give your core group a taster of a typical Youth *Alpha* session. (This has the added advantage of allowing feedback from them before their friends start the course e.g. "If you say *that*, my friends won't come... if you include *this* they will".)

Schools

Most schools should welcome a friendly request to visit. You could offer to do a short assembly to plug the course.

Make sure the head teacher and head of RE have a copy of the course to look through.

If the school has a Christian Union, you could run an *Alpha* course in association with its activities. (Bear in mind that some school CU's tend to put off or intimidate the very young people that you want to attract.)

CREATING THE RIGHT ENVIRONMENT

♦ Whatever room or venue you use, it should be comfortable and the right size for the group. A front living room is great for a small group.

♦ Try not to use a room which is being used for another activity at the same time or which is a through route to somewhere else.

♦ Have something going on as they arrive e.g. music playing, video playing (e.g. video from recent Chart Show) etc.

♦ Make it easy for latecomers to join the group without feeling awkward.

♦ Try not to over-run the session and make sure people can get home/to their next lesson etc. on time.

♦ If you have time, prepare displays and visual aids which will complement the Youth *Alpha* session (e.g. theories which explain the resurrection or newspaper clippings to provoke thought on "What's Wrong with the World?")

GIVING A SHORT TALK

There are many ways in which you can get information across. Sometimes the best way to put over information is simply by giving a short talk.

Preparation

♦ Can you sum up the aim of the talk in one simple sentence? e.g. "By the end of my talk, the young people will have a better understanding of..."

♦ Select key points. What do you want the group to think, do, believe or say differently as a result of the talk?

Structure

♦ *State:* Each new point or heading as clearly and simply as possible.

♦ *Explain:* As short and to the point as possible - Don't waffle!

♦ *Illustrate:* As interesting and relevant as you can make it.

Young people especially think in terms of pictures, images and illustrations, *not* deep theological truths. For example:

"Grace is not earned through works or what you do but is a free gift from God".

is better put across as,

"Imagine your friend won the lottery...and then gave you the lot."

◆ *Apply.* "Yes, but how?" Give the group something practical to go away and work on.

> Work out concrete ways
> to illustrate the following abstract theological points in a way
> that young people will understand and relate to:
> ✝ REPENTANCE ✝ FORGIVENESS ✝ SIN ✝ GRACE ✝ FAITH✝
> Make sure your definitions are free from jargon.

◆ Appeal to their senses, not just to their intellect. Use visual aids to enhance the point you want to make and ensure your language is "teenage-friendly".

> Nothing is taught until something is learnt.

> It is estimated that about 80% of communication is non-verbal.

" He loves you. It says so. "

GIVING A SHORT TESTIMONY

It is always possible to argue over facts. It is impossible to deny someone's personal testimony. We are all intrigued by the way other people choose to live their lives. The young people will be fascinated by insights into your life. It will almost certainly have as great an impact as anything you teach them.

For an even greater impact, interview one of the young people themselves or someone who is just a few years older than them. An interview is less daunting for them than a monologue and enables you to shape the content of what they say.

Either "How I came to Christ" *or* "What Jesus means to me today".

♦ Testimonies should be brief, honest but not shocking, specific and practical.

♦ Make sure that Jesus/God gets the glory rather than your former lifestyle.

♦ Don't preach. Avoid churchy jargon.

♦ Weave in biblical concepts and truths without reading the Bible.

USING FILM AND VIDEO CLIPS

Film or video clips are great for raising questions, setting up an issue or illustrating a point in a dramatic, visual way.

DON'T:

♦ Explain the content of the clip. This will weaken the impact.

♦ Use video clips just as a gimmick.

"Here, the man is obviously."

DO:

♦ Check the film well in advance. Sometimes a clip isn't always as you remember it!

♦ Make sure you (or one of your leaders) have full mastery of the technology before you use it.

♦ Think through how you will introduce the clip and how you will follow it up immediately afterwards.

Copyright: The law is confusing over the use of specific video clips as suggested in this manual. Film and video companies have advised that technically it is illegal to show all or part of a hired film to anyone other than your family. However, in practice the law is extremely difficult to interpret. As no one has ever been taken to court over this issue, there is no established precedent. Normally distribution companies do not mind clips of their films being shown as long as:

♦ It is only a tiny part of the whole film.

♦ No money is changing hands.

♦ No profit is being made.

However, it is good practice to write a letter outlining:

♦ What you plan to show and in what context

♦ That no entrance fee will be made.

Ask them to respond (give a deadline) only if they object. The address of the distribution company should be in the video box.

LEADING SMALL GROUP DISCUSSION

Young people face so many options and choices today. We need to help them make right decisions rather than just know the right answers.

The church's traditional response has been to indoctrinate - to preach and try to yell its point of view louder than the rest of the world.

"It says in Corinthians..."

This will no longer do.

"Telling isn't teaching, listening isn't learning."

Young people have "information overload" from a variety of voices and messages. Most of these have a far greater impact than those they hear from the church. For much of the time they are told what to do, both at school and at home. They are not often actively encouraged to think for themselves.

It is our task to teach young people *how* to think, not just *what* to think. We must equip them to make the right decisions *for themselves*.

There is no better way to encourage learning and discovery than through discussion. When young people are talking about a given subject, they are most likely thinking seriously about it and trying to understand it better.

However, it is good practice to write a letter outlining:

♦ What you plan to show and in what context

♦ That not entrance fee will be made

Ask them to respond (give a deadline) only if they object. The address of the distribution company should be in the video box.

If young people are to make a meaningful response to the gospel, then we need to provide the necessary information and a forum for logical and direct discussion.

Discussion helps truth rise to the surface. This makes it easier for young people to discover it for themselves.

We need to pray that their hearts and minds will be open to the Holy Spirit's guidance and prompting (John 16:13). we also need to pray for opportunities to show that the Bible can be their guide and that God does have something to say that applies to them.

If young people are to make a meaningful response to the gospel, then we need to provide the necessary information and a forum for logical and direct discussion.

Discussion helps truth rise to the surface. This makes it easier for young people to discover it for themselves.

We need to pray that their hearts and minds will be open to the Holy Spirit's guidance and prompting (John 16:13). We also need to pray for opportunities to show that the Bible can be their guide and that God does have something to say that applies to them.

ASKING QUESTIONS

With reference to young people, our main task as leaders of Youth *Alpha* is to

light fires rather than fill buckets.

The best way to facilitate this is to ask questions.

Questions help to stir imagination. Questions serve to broaden horizons. Questions provoke. Questions create a reaction.

"Who can tell me the hermeneutical and eschatological implications of the Pauline letters...?"

Prepare and ask

♦ Short, uncomplicated questions.

♦ Open questions (questions that cannot be answered with a simple yes or no!) e.g. How?... Why?... What?... To what extent?...

♦ Questions that respect the value and opinions of the individual.

♦ Questions that point to the authority of Scripture.

OPEN QUESTIONS...

...allow a full range of answers, there is not necessarily one "right" answer.

...allow every member of the group to chip in with an answer, not just the group theologian.

...help shy members of the group to find their voice without fear of getting it "wrong".

...establish an early pattern that all contributions are valid and to be encouraged.

OTHER QUESTIONS:

What other ways are there of thinking about this?

Why do you think the Bible says this?

What do you think this means?

What other ideas do people have?

How does this apply to your life?

_DO:_

♦ Visualise the group as you prepare your questions. Make the questions as relevant to their world as possible.

♦ Affirm responses equally, if possible. e.g. "Yes" or "Thank you". This shows you also welcome more responses from others.

♦ Use questions to summarise and apply what you have studied.

DON'T:

♦ Ask a question and then answer it yourself. This devalues the question you have just asked.

♦ Be afraid to challenge gently or to tease out a response - e.g. "Can you explain what you mean by that?" or "Can you give an example?"

♦ Be afraid of silence. Allow time for the group to think about question/issues raised. Allowing silence shows that you value thoughtful and considered responses.

It might be helpful to comment "It's a difficult issue, isn't it?" or "It's hard to be the first one to talk". This could help if the silence feels awkward.

USING THE BIBLE

♦ Use a modern translation. Always give page numbers to help them find their way about.

♦ Do not assume that they are familiar with the Bible, its culture, style, layout, well known stories etc. Try to give a brief introduction to any passage of Scripture that you use.

♦ Do not give the impression that using the list of contents is inferior.

♦ Do not assume that all members of the group are happy to read aloud or, indeed, that they can read.

♦ If you want a group member to read aloud, always check with them first. Let the rest of the group know that you have done this. Then they will not worry that you might spring the next reading on them.

♦ Even if everyone is happy to read aloud, avoid reading round the group. It is far better to have one person read the whole passage.

LEADERS' ROLE WITH THE SMALL GROUP

♦ Become a "facilitator". A facilitator is simply another member of the group who is helping to make the discussion happen. We are not sitting in judgement on the young people or their responses. We are looking to guide and steer the group rather than dictate terms or indoctrinate the young people.

♦ Look for opinions not answers. e.g. ask what the young people *feel* or *think*. The words "Do you think?" makes the question a matter of opinion rather than a matter of knowing the right answer.

♦ Foster an environment of open discussion. The young people will feel like it is their group. As a result they are much more likely to hold on to what they have discovered and learnt.

Remember that ultimately we do not want to produce mere compliant, passive converts. We want to ignite and nurture active disciples, who will then go out and reach other people of their own accord.

A facilitator will:

Affirm all legitimate opinions.

Actively listen to each person.

Not force anyone to talk.

Not take sides during the discussion.

Be creative and flexible...know what the goals are for each discussion/session.

Briefly summarise key points that have been made.

If the group tends to direct all their questions to you, affirm the questioner and then gently redirect the question back to the group.

e.g. "That's a thoughtful question, thank you. I wonder what some of you think." or "How would you attempt to answer that?".

GROUND RULES FOR AN EFFECTIVE DISCUSSION

♦ No put-downs. Mutual respect is important. It is permissible for the group to attack *ideas,* but not *each other.*

♦ There's no such thing as a stupid question. It is vital that the young people feel free to ask questions at any time. Asking questions is an indication that they want to learn.

♦ No one is forced to talk and only one person talks at a time. This is a good way to teach young people mutual respect. If each person's opinion is worthwhile, it deserves to be heard.

MINISTRY

John Wimber has defined ministry as "meeting the needs of others on the basis of God's resources."

Values

Youth *Alpha* is not simply a series of plausible arguments or a neat academic exercise. Young people need to *experience* the fulness of God's Holy Spirit. Young people are capable of being very open to God and of having as deep a relationship with God as adults have. Often we are at fault for not giving them sufficient skills or information to be able to respond fully to God. If young people are to be part of God's kingdom today, we should begin to expect them to have some of the spiritual experiences that adults have.

However, it is important to remember that they can be vulnerable and open to suggestion. It is also important not to underestimate the power and influence of peer pressure (e.g. "she prophesies, I don't, therefore I'm no good, God doesn't love me").

Any experience of God should go hand in hand with the encouragement to live their lives according to God's principles in the Bible. We should stress the fruit of the Spirit over and above experiences and manifestations (Galations 5: 22-23). We need to encourage young people to look at the way they live their lives so that they are able to recognise the long-term effect of the Holy Spirit in their lives.

God is at work in each of our lives because he has promised to be. We should discourage young people from believing that God is only present when we feel able to prove that he is - by strange phenomena.

Ministry is the work of the Holy Spirit, not of the individual praying. We sometimes tend to protect young people from ministry because we can recall examples of bad practice.

If each of us had no examples in our mind of bad practice, we would be far more responsive to God when he blesses young people anyway.

A Simple Model for Ministry

♦ Pray in a relaxed manner.

♦ Take time to sort out any difficulties of belief and assurance. e.g. Am I ready? Will God really bless me?

♦ Ensure that the young people know what is going to happen (as far as you are able to tell them) and tell them how you are going to pray. Males with males, females with females or mixed groupings.

♦ Encourage their faith. Read a promise of God from the Bible, tell them of your own experience, or better still get another young person to tell the group what happened to them when they were filled with the Holy Spirit. Again, beware of suggestion. Testimonies of "fruit" are better than those of "manifestation". (eg. "...and now I really get on with my Dad and I am trying not to slag people off at school...")

- Stay facing the person you are praying for and ask the Holy Spirit to come. Welcome him if you see signs that he is working. Wait on God as you pray for further directions from him.

- Silently ask God what he wants to do or say. Ask him to show you how to encourage the young people you pray with.

- Ask them what they think is happening. Prompt them but try not to put pressure on them. Always give young people a "get-out clause". e.g. "Do you sense God might be saying something? Maybe God is painting a picture in your mind for you. Don't worry if not."

- Keep talking about the ministry time with the young people. Keep in touch with those who felt that they experienced something *and* with those who felt that they did not.

- Pray for them regularly.

DO:

- All that you can to retain the dignity of the individual.

- Have at least one person of the same sex praying with each individual.

- Explain everything as simply as possible. Try to de-mystify your language and make it jargon free. Be yourself, be natural, try not to slip into "spiritual minister" mode.

- Encourage the individuals you are praying for.

- Use Biblical authority.

- Answer their questions but try not to fill them with ideas or suggestions.

♦ Reflect any questions you may ask them back onto God rather than the individual. e.g. "What is God showing you in your picture?" rather than, "What do you see in your picture?"

♦ Keep in close touch with church leaders and parents. Within the church, it is worth remembering that youth ministry is a delegated ministry. Parents have the ultimate God given responsibility. (Deuteronomy 11:18-21, Proverbs 22:6, Ephesians 4:6)

♦ Encourage them to weigh up any words or pictures very carefully (see 1Thessalonians 5:19-22), to talk to other respected leaders and/or parents.

♦ Be aware that young people often have a high degree of trust and relatively low ability (through inexperience of life only) to discern.

♦ Be prepared to take ultimate responsibility for any words of knowledge or prophecy that are given. e.g. "I sense that God might want to say...but I could be wrong. Do you want to think and pray about it and see if you agree? You may want to talk to someone else and see what they think. Don't worry if you don't think it is what God is saying. Do get back to me about it."

♦ Remember that the effects of ministry may not be seen by us for some time.

♦ Encourage young people to seek long-term fruit (John 15:16) rather than a short-term "high".

DON'T:

♦ Pressurise young people into anything they do not want to do.

♦ Pray on your own with a young person.

♦ Leave the room where the group is praying in order to pray individually with a young person .

♦ Touch individuals inappropriately.

♦ Feel that you have to apologise for God or explain everything on his behalf. If God is at work, the young people will know that for themselves.

EVALUATION

Evaluation is both a process and an event. It is vital that you keep in touch with your team and ask them how they feel the course is going. Don't be afraid to ask the young people themselves. (e.g. "Did you find the last session helpful?" or "what are you enjoying most about the sessions so far?")

Always be prepared to act on what you hear.

At the end of the course invite the young people to fill in a simple evaluation sheet.

> Think back over all the Youth *Alpha* sessions. Complete the following statements:
>
> The best thing about Youth *Alpha* was...
>
> Youth *Alpha* would be even better if...
>
> I would like to have more teaching on...

Make the sheets anonymous, this will encourage honest feedback.

Encourage your Youth *Alpha* team as well as the Church leadership, prayer groups etc. with the results of the evaluation.

Take time to reflect on the course and any subsequent feedback you receive. Allow enough time to discuss, pray, plan and implement any changes that need to be made before you run the course again.

FINALLY

"If someone does not believe in God, they don't believe in nothing, they believe in anything!" (G K Chesterton)

Young people today are as spiritually hungry as ever before. Yet they are continually sold lies and given half truths everywhere they turn. They want to believe something. They are encouraged to believe anything. They often end up feeling trapped and confused.

Youth *Alpha* contains the truth of the gospel. Be encouraged as you prepare, teach and lead each session. Be prayerful and committed to the young people you come across. Work hard at presenting the sessions to young people. Then they will know the truth, and the truth will set them free (See John 8:32).

A TYPICAL YOUTH ALPHA SESSION

A BRIEF SCHEDULE

Pray with Youth *Alpha* leaders

Prepare and lay out the room   10 - 15 mins

People arrive and are welcomed   5 mins

Introductory activity/icebreaker   5 - 10 mins

Worship   10 mins

Main Session including:
video clips   15 - 20 mins
visual aids
talk with illustration and
application (where appropriate)

Small group discussion   10 - 15 mins

End of Session   5 mins

Total   60 - 80 mins

Before the Session Starts

♦ Have something going on. It always helps young people to feel a little less awkward or shy if there is something to do, watch or listen to. Either some music playing (encourage them to bring their own) or a video playing (e.g. "Sport gone crazy", "Speed gone crazy", "It'll be alright on the Night" etc.).

♦ Have some quotes, statistics, statements or questions displayed on the wall or an OHP.

♦ Have some visual aids. For example, a picture of a chain snapping free or a simple picture of the cross.

♦ Have some snacks and drinks available e.g. popcorn, coke etc. Tell them to help themselves.

♦ Do everything you can to make sure that individuals in the group feel as comfortable as possible. Do they know where the loo is? Do they know what time the session will end?

♦ Ask your "core" group to arrive ten minutes early. This ensures that there are some young people, as well as yourself, around as others arrive.

THE START OF THE SESSION

Welcome people warmly and introduce the Youth *Alpha* course and the session as briefly as possible. It is like a bus journey. The group don't need to know every street but they may not be willing to board the bus at all if they don't know the general direction it is going.

Young people tend to shy away from "courses". Say something like: "Hi! welcome to *Alpha*. *Alpha* is a series of ten sessions to look at some of the things Christians believe. It is open to anyone, it doesn't matter if you have never thought seriously about Christianity before... Do ask questions... This session we're going to look at...Who is Jesus?"

Each section on a Youth *Alpha* session should last no more than fifteen minutes. (Studies show that the maximum concentration span of an adult is 18 minutes for any one activity).

Try to involve as many people as possible throughout each session. Have helpers to:

1. Turn on/ turn off lights for video, OHP etc.
2. Operate the video.
3. Operate the OHP.
4. Hand out sheets and pens etc.

The more individual members feel that they have a part to play, the more inclined they will be to want to come next time.

ICEBREAKERS, GAMES AND ACTIVITIES

Icebreakers can help self-conscious teenagers by creating a way in which the young people can discover things they have in common. Icebreakers are a way of bonding people together. Once young people feel they have something in common with other members of the group, they are far more likely to share their ideas and reveal their true feelings to each other.

Icebreakers should be fun but not pointless. The best icebreakers are easy to set up and explain. They don't last too long and are quick and easy to bring to an end.

Some Simple Icebreakers

Questions

♦ If you knew that tomorrow was the last day of your life, how would you spend the day?

♦ If you were given £5000 and told you had to spend it all in a week, how would you spend it?

Games or activities

◆ *Dingbats.* Popular game easily available. It is essentially "written" Charades. If you were doing a session on "How does God Guide us", you could end the icebreaker and lead into the rest of the session by saying "...that game requires a different or new way of thinking about things. It helps to try and see things from a different perspective when we look at how God guides us..."

◆ *Articulate.* Players have to describe as many objects, people or places to a team mate in a fixed time without actually naming the particular object, person or place in question.

◆ Have a pile of wacky or outrageous clothes. Divide the group into teams. Set up a relay race, where the first person runs to the pile of clothes puts on at least three items and another member of the team takes a photo of them. They then take off the clothes and run back. The next person then goes and repeats the process. Develop the film for the next session. You could use the photos as a fashion contest for an icebreaker next week. This icebreaker may not work well with older or more sophisticated teenagers.

◆ Ask the individuals "If you were a...(cartoon character, animal or car) what one would you be and why?" This helps the individuals to reveal a bit about themselves to the rest of the group without them feeling that they are actually talking about themselves.

◆ Video one of the popular soaps on TV particularly an ending where a decision has to be made and the plot is up in the air. Play this to the group and ask them what will/should happen next.

◆ Ask the group how they would spend a typical night out. Assign each corner of the room as a plausible answer (e.g. See a film;

- go out for a meal; hang out in the market square; go round to a friend's house). Allow a minute or two for the group to chat to the people they find in the same corner as them. Then get them to have a quick look at who is in the other corners.

- Give them several other options to choose, e.g. evening in, Scrabble with the family, homework, TV, on the phone to friends. TV programme e.g. Morse, Beavis and Butthead, a BBC 2 documentary or an action packed film.

- Get each member of the group to read out three statements about themselves - two of them must be true and one of them must be false. The rest of the group have to guess which is the false statement.

- Get hold of a tape of "It'll be alright on the night". Play some of the clips and stop the tape just before the "disaster" - ask them to guess "what happened next".

WORSHIP

It may not be appropriate to have worship at the first few Youth *Alpha* sessions (or for the whole course). On the other hand, it may be a good opportunity to introduce alternative forms of praise and worship.

It is worth bearing in mind that singing is considered to be extremely naff and uncool by most teenagers. Adolescent boys are struggling with a voice that is breaking and only "nerds" sing in school assembly (not many secondary schools regularly attempt a hymn in assembly today). However, it is perfectly possible to get round this and still encourage the young people towards an attitude of worship.

Alternative ideas for Worship include

♦ Have a credible worship tape playing (e.g. DC Talk, Cutting Edge). Display some Bible verses or a short Bible passage.

♦ Have some instrumental music playing and read some relevant Bible verses, devotional passages or some poetry by Christian artists.

♦ It is possible to hire or buy devotional videos (though be sure to check them out first. They must not be naff!)

♦ After doing one of the above, if it is appropriate, ask the group if they would like to respond in some way. This may be by saying a short prayer of thanks or praise. (It is good for you to "model" this - no jargon, keep it brief.)

♦ You could create a Psalm. Each group member writes down two words or phrases that came into their mind as they were listening and watching. Compile these words and phrases together to make a group Psalm of thanks and praise.

SAMPLE SESSION 1:

WHO IS JESUS?

Begin by welcoming everyone. Explain briefly what Youth *Alpha* is and briefly what you hope that the group will have covered by the end of the course.

Why are they famous?

Use "The Guinness Book of Records", especially the human achievements section, to produce a fun quiz. The group have to try and guess what extraordinary feat the individuals you select have achieved. e.g. Neil Armstrong - First man on the moon. Roger Bannister - First person to run a mile in under 4 minutes. Michael Faraday - First man to produce an electric current from a magnetic field. Rebecca Stephens - First British woman to climb Mount Everest. Camelot - First company to organise the National Lottery.

Make the point that these people made extremely significant break-throughs which have an impact on each of our lives today. Jesus Christ had the biggest impact of all on human life.

Jesus was fully human

Choose one or two examples and illustrate them. e.g. Jesus was tempted (Mark 1:13). We often feel tempted and we can often feel that temptation can be overpowering. Jesus understands how we feel because he was tempted too.

What did Jesus say about himself?

Jesus was more than just a man. He made claims about himself.

Choose one of the things that Jesus said about himself and illustrate it. e.g. Light of the World (John 8:12) To illustrate this you could black out the room and turn off the lights or ask anyone who remembers the last time they were in a power cut on a dark evening. Trees need light in order to produce oxygen by the process of photosynthesis. Jesus described himself as *the light of the world.*

Jesus also said

Jesus said things which challenge us to make a response. Choose an example and illustrate it. A short personal testimony might be appropriate at this point.

Ultimately Jesus claimed to be the Son of God.

But several people have made similar claims. e.g. David Icke - Son of God (c.1991) or David Koresh - Lamb of God(1993)

David Icke, David Koresh, Jesus... "Mad, Bad or God" ?

The Evidence

Focus especially on the fulfilment of Old Testement prophecy and the Resurrection.

Small Group Questions/Activities

If Jesus appeared at your school tomorrow, where do you think you would find him? In the school yard? Behind the bike shed? In the staff room? In the back row of the classroom or in the front row?

SAMPLE SESSION 2:

WHY DID JESUS DIE?

Begin by welcoming the group, especially anyone who is new.

Briefly introduce the session and say what you hope to have covered by the end of it.

Either. Ask who wears a cross on a chain round their neck or has earrings in the shape of a cross?

Make the point that the cross lies at the heart of the Christian faith.

Or. show a short clip of the crucifixion from *Jesus of Nazareth.*

Mankind's greatest need

Either: What's in the news?
Hand out relevant pages, leader columns, picture stories etc. from newspapers and ask the groups briefly to summarise what is wrong with the world today, using the articles as examples. Use this to lead into the talk.

Or: show the group a slide picture. When it's projected, you see on the wall a perfect representation of what's on the film. In the same way, when we were created, we were a perfect representation of God's character - we were made in his image.

Now twist the lens. The picture becomes blurred and finally unrecognisable. Explain, that is what sin does, blur the image of God in people. Use this as an illustration in the talk.

Talk
Sin spoils...God's creation
Sin spreads...throughout the world
Sin separates...us from God

Include Bible verses e.g. Isaiah 53:6 or Romans 3:23.

Make the point that mankind's greatest need is forgiveness.

What God has done

If you have time, show a video clip from *"Coming to America"*
An African prince gives up his claim to the throne in Africa, becomes a cleaner in America in order to win his true love. Show the scene towards the end of the film where he explains to his bride-to-be, on the underground train, what he did and why he did it.

Make the point that God sent Jesus to be a substitute for us.

What the Cross achieved

Choose one "P" in the Youth *Alpha* notes and illustrate it. e.g. Penalty - the Law Court - tell the story of the judge and the criminal. (You could invite two people from the group to act out the story as a role play.)

Either: End by playing an appropriate song (e.g. "Living Lord") and allow time for personal prayer. You could use the prayer at the end of the *Why Jesus?* booklet as an example of a typical prayer.

Or: Show a clip from *"Indiana Jones and the Last Crusade"* - Final dramatic scene - penitent men bow before the breath of God. Walk in the steps of God. Take a step of faith.

Use this to help explain how someone can become a Christian.

Small Group Questions

Either: How would you feel if: A friend gave you £50 without wanting it back at any stage?

Or: A friend at school offered to own up for a serious offence which *you* had committed?

SAMPLE SESSION 3:

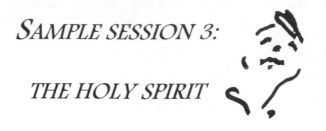

THE HOLY SPIRIT

The three sessions on the Holy Spirit could be incorporated into a weekend away with the young people.

A weekend away would provide the opportunity to relax and get to know each young person individually. It removes the pressure of having to squeeze a Youth *Alpha* session into a fixed period of time. It also provides the opportunity for the young people to get to know you properly and not just as the "leader".

If a weekend is not a realistic option, then a day together can work equally as well. (e.g. at a local Theme Park, Adventure Centre or simply a different venue from normal, such as someone's house) Top and tail the day with two or three sessions on the Holy Spirit.

Here is a way in which you could run all three sessions on the Holy Spirit into one session.

WHO IS THE HOLY SPIRIT?

Either: Ask people what immediately comes into their minds when you say "The Holy Spirit". Discuss their responses.

Or: Before the meeting, cut out pictures from newspapers and magazines of a wide variety of famous people and put them up round the room. A group member could help you choose some that the group will know.

Ask the group to look at the different pictures and to choose the person they most like. They could stand by the one they have chosen.

Divide the group into pairs and ask them to say one way in which they wish they were like that person, and one way in which they are glad to be different from them. If you have a very small group, do this together.

You could then ask them to say one way in which they would like to be like Jesus.

Make the point that part of the Holy Spirit's work is to change us to be more like Jesus.

In the Old /New Testament

Introduce The Holy Spirit by referring briefly to

♦ His work in Creation.

♦ His equipping particular people at particular times (choose one example).

♦ The promise that he would come in a new way.

Read selected passages from Acts 2. Explain that this fulfilled the Old Testement promises.

WHAT DOES THE HOLY SPIRIT DO?

Choose two or three of the following references and illustrate them to show what the Holy Spirit does.

John 3:5-6

John 1:12

Romans 8:15-17

Galatians 5:22-23

Romans 12:6-8

For example, *Either:* Bring in your birth certificate and say how this proves that you were born and that your parents were x and y. Then read John 3:6 to show how The Holy Spirit gives us new birth into God's family. Link this with John1:12 to show how we become God's children.

Or: Ask if any of the group have ever been compared, in terms of looks or mannerisms, to another member of their immediate family. Read Galatians 5:22-23 to show how The Holy Spirit produces a "family likeness" in God's family. (Stress that bearing spiritual fruit is a good thing just in case they feel ambivalent about looking like their brothers or sisters!)

HOW CAN I BE FILLED WITH THE HOLY SPIRIT?

The Vacuum Experiment

Take a large plastic lemonade bottle and screw the top on tight. Place the bottle in a bowl of hot water (alternatively under a hot water tap for a minute or so). Then take it out and place it either in a fridge or under a cold tap, or if it is a cold night even on the window ledge, for at least a couple of minutes. When the air inside the bottle is heated it expands and then when it is cooled it rapidly contracts. The pressure outside the bottle is then too great and the bottle crumples inwards!

Make the point that we need to be filled to be strong.

Explain that the Bible tells us that every Christian has the Holy Spirit (Romans 8:9) but that not every Christian is filled with the Holy Spirit.

♦ The Bible also commands us to be filled with the Spirit (Ephesians 5:18)

♦ So how can I be filled ?

♦ Ask!! Luke 11:9-13

♦ A short testimony could be helpful at this point, especially if it is from one of the young people themselves.

♦ Use an illustration of your own to show how God loves to give, we only have to ask. It might be good to stress that it does not matter how old you are. You don't have to be on the Parish Church Council (PCC) before you are eligible to receive the Holy Spirit. The promise is for everyone. (Acts 2:17 or Joel 2:28 compare it with Joel 2:16)

- On a small sheet or card, prepare a checklist to cover:
  How can I be filled with the Holy Spirit?
  (desire, ask, co-operate, believe, persevere)

- What stops us being filled with the Holy Spirit?
  (doubt, fear, unworthiness)

- Allow enough time at the end of the session to give anyone who
  wants it the opportunity to be prayed for.

SMALL GROUP DISCUSSION

Allow enough time for discussion within each session (minimum time 8-10 minutes). A discussion can work with two or three people. It is probably best with a group of about six to eight. A large group can be split down into smaller groups. However, if you lack sufficient leaders, it is better to have a big group effectively led than small, intimate groups that go wrong.

How to Stimulate Successful Small Group Discussions

The small group discussions on *Alpha* require quite a high degree of abstract, cerebral thought. This can seem quite daunting, not least to young people. Most young people have not fully developed the ability to "think on their feet". They find it hard to organise their thoughts spontaneously and with confidence. They are afraid to speak for fear that they might sound stupid.

It is therefore vital that we allow them time to interact with the subject matter in an interesting, challenging and thought-provoking way *before* the actual discussion begins.

Once young people have had a chance to organise their thoughts, many of them actually can't wait to contribute and listen to others.

♦ Tell a story, get the group to identify with the characters. People love stories about other people. Look how many people tune into the "soaps" each week on TV.

♦ Read a passage from a book or magazine article. Summarise the main points. Begin by asking, "To what extent do you agree with this view...?", or, "If you were to give this opinion a mark out of 10, what mark would you give it... and why?"

♦ Play a well known chart song dealing with the theme. Many contemporary artists reveal a deep searching or longing within their songwriting. (e.g. Queen: "Is this the world we created?" or "This could be Heaven for everyone" or Michael Jackson: "Earth Song") Copy the lyrics out for the group so that they can study them more closely. (These are easy to obtain from Smash Hits magazine).

♦ With some young people it may be possible to create a skit or role play which covers a particular issue linked with the session. Invite the young people to take part, but make it easy for anyone who does not want to take part. Brainstorm alternative options or endings based on a key decision made in the role play. Get the group to vote on an option and then get them to role play the consequences of choosing that option. If there is time (and inclination) get them to role play the consequence of the options they voted against. Discuss the various outcomes.

♦ Present some current statistics or survey results. Try to get the group to compare and contrast facts and figures. Ask them for opinions on differences/similarities.

♦ Use posters, slides or other visual aids (perhaps in conjunction with a song - see above) to concentrate the focus on a particular theme.

♦ Ask: "What immediately comes into your mind when I say...?" Brainstorm and then evaluate the responses.

♦ Deal out some cards to each member of the group with relevant or challenging statements written on them (e.g. "Jesus never existed"; "Some of the Bible is unreliable"). Invite a member of the group to place a card in the middle of the group so that everyone can read it. Ask people to respond. If there is no response, ask the person who dealt the card to say why they chose that one. At an appropriate time (just *before* it threatens to drag on) ask someone to deal a new card.

This method allows the young people time to form an initial response themselves before they speak to the group. It also allows you to set the pace and length of the discussion time.

♦ Agree/disagree. One end of the room is "I totally agree with this" and the other end of the room is "That's ridiculous, I totally disagree!" Ask the group to imagine a line between the two extremes and to stand somewhere on the line each time you

read out statements, quotations etc. Invite anyone who is willing to say why they have stood where they are. Alternatively, give them 2 minutes to try to get more people to stand with them (using words rather than force).

♦ Vox pop. Use a camcorder/tape recorder to record people in your church, down your street, at the shops, in the bus queue etc. to give their views on a topic. e.g. "Do you ever pray?" Keep it short and fast moving. No sermons! As a rough indication, watch and time how long trailers for programmes on TV take. See how much information and stimulation can be packed into 30 seconds.

Even the most weighty news item on TV gets little more than 5 minutes. (Do not be put off by the professionals. The young people will not mind poor quality, especially if they have been involved with filming and producing it).

♦ Get the group to produce something as a result of their discussion. A manifesto - "Living as a Christian means..." or an advert to attract people to the church or the next Youth *Alpha* course. Encourage them to suggest ideas, listen to others, evaluate contributions etc.

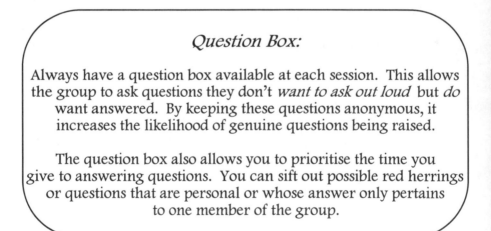

Question Box:

Always have a question box available at each session. This allows the group to ask questions they don't *want to ask out loud* but *do* want answered. By keeping these questions anonymous, it increases the likelihood of genuine questions being raised.

The question box also allows you to prioritise the time you give to answering questions. You can sift out possible red herrings or questions that are personal or whose answer only pertains to one member of the group.

THE END OF EACH SESSION

Have coffee/drinks and snacks available. Put some music back on. Both these are more conducive to chat. Very often it is not until the end of the session that some young people choose to "open up".

Ask individual members of the group to help you pack things away. This also gives you an opportunity to talk one-to-one with members of the group.

FINALLY

Don't worry if you don't cover everything. Don't force feed them. It is good to leave them wanting more.

Trust the Holy Spirit. It is tempting to despair at what young people seem to forget! Equally, it is sometimes amazing what they remember.

OTHER RESOURCES

Outside In - Mike Breen

A practical workbook full of things to do to make effective work among unchurched young people become a reality.
Published by Scripture Union.

The Christian Youth Manual - Steve Chalke

An excellent resource for anyone wanting to start work among young people. It includes an introduction to modern pressures including abuse, family pressures, HIV and AIDS. There is also a thorough checklist of resources and ideas. Published by Kingsway.

Youth Work and How to do it - Pete Ward, Sam Adams and Jude Levermore

A great resource which offers training and practical insight into areas of youth culture, personal skills, group dynamics and worship. Published by Lynx Communications.

YOUTHWORK Magazine

Published bi-monthly, this magazine has resources and ideas, ready-to-use meeting guides as well as relevant features on all aspects of youth ministry. Published by Elm House Christian Communications.

YOUTHWORK Ready-to-Use Meeting Guides

Compiled by John Buckeridge. Several volumes each containing creative and fun session plans with photocopiable activity worksheets. Published by Kingsway.

UCCF - Getting Creative booklet and packs

These are full of helpful and creative ideas for preparing to stage user friendly, evangelistic events. These are a particularly useful source of quotes, video ideas, poems and readings. They are all available from: UCCF, 38 De Montford Street, Leicester, LE1 7GP.

Whose Life is it Anyway? - A beginners' guide to Christianity

Written by Andy Hickford, this covers the Christian basics for young people today. It is cringe-free but solid Biblical teaching - essential for new Christians. This is an ideal follow-up course for young people after they have done Youth *Alpha*.

Hands On - Making Confirmation Count

Produced by CPAS. Although this is designed to prepare young people for confirmation, it is an excellent resource which can easily be adapted to fit young people with a wide range of Christian experience, personality, social background and ability.

You're Only Young Once - YOYO

Compiled by Peter Graystone, Paul Sharpe and Pippa Turner. These are a whole series of group Bible study resources for over thirteens. Again very easy to adapt as each session has material which can be presented in three different styles or approaches. Produced by Scripture Union.

High School Talk Sheets

Compiled by David Lynn, these creative discussions for teenage youth groups cover a whole range of issues and subjects. They never fail to get some kind of discussion going with young people. Produced by Zondervan Publishing House.

IDEAS FOR YOUTH ALPHA SESSIONS

The following is intended as a selection of possible activities for each of the Youth *Alpha* sessions. They are only meant as suggestions and are not meant to be prescriptive in any way. They are included because they have proved to be effective. However, something that works well with one group of young people may prove to be a disaster with a different group. Therefore, these activities should be chosen carefully, always with your group (and individuals within your group) in mind. Always be prepared to adapt and tailor them to suit the needs and ability of your group.

Mismatching group and activities could have a very negative effect on the whole Youth *Alpha* course. It is so important that you and your team know or understand (or both) the particular group of young people you are working with.

SOME CONSIDERATIONS

♦ *Age.* There can be a vast difference between a 12 year old and an 18 year old.

♦ *Maturity.* There can be a significant difference between two 14 year olds.

♦ *Single Sex or Mixed.* This can create a very different tone and requires different treatment and approach.

The relationships within the group. How well do the individuals in the group know each other? Will they feel self-conscious with a "wacky" icebreaker? If they know each other well, is there any need for an icebreaker?

Academic ability. Are they used to discussion?

Length of each session. A 40 minute school lunch break will require short, concise activities.

The stage of the course. You may not need to have an icebreaker for session 10. Equally, you may need to have activities that allow for more individual responses if individuals in the group have progressed at different rates.

The spiritual state of the group. A group that are eager and "spiritually hungry" will want more time for questions, discussion and prayer. Equally, you may need to have plenty of activities up your sleeve for a group who are only able to take a little spiritual input at a time.

WHO IS JESUS?

Video Clip

"Forrest Gump" Forrest Gump runs across America "for no particular reason". He builds up a large following of people. He suddenly stops and makes his way home.

Make the point that all of us follow something or someone (Pop star, fashion, sports heroes...). Do we know *why* we are following them?

Icebreakers

Where are they now?

Stick up pictures or photographs of famous people. e.g. Madonna, Harrison Ford, Bono, John Major. See how many of the group can name them. Ask how many would be remembered in 20 years time or 200 or 2,000.

Make the point that these people are famous now, but how long will their fame last?

✖ Identikit

Use this as an Icebreaker. You will need to collect at least 25 photographs of very well-known pop-stars, sportsmen/women, TV/film personalities/actors, etc. Because their faces are so well known make it a bit harder to identify the person by cutting out just a small part of their face (e.g. eyes and nose) and then display these around the walls of the venue/room. With a pad and pencil, the young people need to identify the stars from the photofit section of face shown.

Make the point that they are well known *now* but who would remember them in 200 years time, let alone 2000 years.

✠Meek and Mild

Collect a selection of pictures and illustrations depicting Jesus. These could include Christmas cards, postcards of oil paintings, religious pictures and statues. Ask the young people to comment on the pictures and give and opinion of the sort of person these images portray.

Make the point that Jesus is considered by many to have been a wimpy, white-faced, blue-eyed man who wore a white sheet and ended up a victim. The Bible does not portray him like that at all!

Small group activity

❧*Jesus Who?* (See page 62) Ask the group to fill in the sheet and then use this as a springboard for discussion.

Small group questions

◆ What do you think of when people talk about God? In what ways has looking at Jesus changed your impression?

◆ If Jesus lived today on earth, what do you think he would:
Wear?
Say?
Do?
Watch on TV?
Think about the things he would see on the news or in the papers?

◆ Jesus - mad, bad or God? What do you think and why?

◆ If you had a chance to meet Jesus, what would you *say* to him? What would you *ask* him? What would you like *him* to say to you?

"He lived many years ago."

"He was a good man."

"LIKE A VICAR"

"Great teacher"

"A swear word."

"Someone to joke about"

"He's alive."

"He died, but came alive again."

Yes   don't know   NO

WHY DID JESUS DIE?

Video Clips

"Jesus of Nazareth" Show an appropriate clip from this classic film.

"Coming to America" An African prince gives up his claim to the throne in Africa and becomes a cleaner in America in order to win his true love. Scene towards the end of the film where he explains to his bride-to-be, on the underground train, what he did and why he did it.

"Indiana Jones and the Last Crusade" The final dramatic scene - where penitent men bow before the breath of God. Walk in the steps of God. Take a step of faith.

"The Mission" The scene where Robert De Niro has a huge weight of armour cut away by the natives he used to hunt. Powerful display of forgiveness.

Discussion Starter

Change the World. On a big sheet of paper draw a large circle (e.g. round a washing up bowl) to represent the world. Ask the group, in twos or threes, to write their suggestions for improving the world within the circle. They can draw symbols instead of writing (e.g. draw a tree with a line through it to represent 'preserve the rainforest'). Discuss their solutions.

Make the point that Christians believe that the cross provides the ultimate solution to the human problem.

Icebreaker

What's in the news?

Hand out relevant pages, leader columns, picture stories etc. from newspapers and ask the groups briefly to summarise what is wrong with the world today. Ask them to come up with possible solutions.

Make the point that mankind's greatest need is forgiveness.

❧ Father And Son

Four men in a straight line.

A: My name is Anthony Menzies. My father is Sir James Menzies, the banker.
B: My name is Martin Brown. My father is Stephen Brown, an accountant.
C: I'm Lee Alcock. I dunno who my father is.
D: I am the voice you cannot silence. My Father created the world.
A: I was conceived in my parents' holiday villa in Italy.
B: I was conceived in the house in which I now live, on my parents' third wedding anniversary.
C: I was conceived in a hedge behind The Three Crowns. The pub's been knocked down now.
D: I was conceived by a miracle. My mother was a virgin.
B: I was born in Surbiton maternity hospital, Greater London.
C: I was born on a number 48 bus somewhere between Balham and the terminus.
A: I was born in a hotel in the Middle East while my parents were there on a business tour.
D: I was born nearby, in the back yard of a similar hotel.
A: I don't think I like this conversation.
B: I don't think I mind.
C: I don't think.
D: I am.

A: I take after my family. I am tall, muscular and need to shave more often than most. My mother was just like that.

B: I like to think you can see the best of my father in me.

C: I wish I knew what my father was like.

D: I came to show the world the truth of my Father.

B: My father loved me and sent me into business.

A: My father loved me and sent me to public school.

C: If my father had loved me I wouldn't have been sent to Wormwood Scrubs.

D: My Father loved mankind so much that he sent me to show them.

A: I think my father loves me, although he has never had much time to spend with me.

B: I think my father loves me, although I was scared of him when I was young.

C: Strange way my father had of loving me, abandoning me to die.

D: (*Pause*) Strange indeed!

A: I would fight for the truth.

B: I would fight for my country.

C: I'd fight anyone for a laugh!

D: I laid down my life without fighting.

A: My father said to me: 'You're going to grow up a fine representative of the family tradition.'

B: My father said to me: 'You're going to grow up to be just like... your mother.'

C: My father never said nothing, but I know what I'd like to say to him.

D: My Father said: 'This is my Son whom I dearly love. I am well pleased with him.'

A: You can meet my father if you make an appointment.

B: I'll introduce you to my father if you like.

C: I wish someone would introduce me to my father.

D: No one comes to the Father except through me.

C: Anyone out there want to adopt me?

Small Group Questions

♦ What do you think about sin? Is it too old fashioned to talk seriously about sin today? How would you explain what sin is to someone who had never heard about it?

♦ Agree/disagree; "Some sins are more serious than others." "If sin does not hurt anyone, it is not really a sin." "God will always forgive our sin" etc...

♦ What do you make of Jesus paying the death penalty instead of you?

Bible Study

Isaiah 53:1-12

In what ways does Jesus fulfil this Old Testement prophecy?

e.g.   v2 no majesty.
         v4 stricken by God.
         v5 pierced, punishment...was upon him.
         v7 silent before accusers.
         v12 crucified with thieves

What do these verses teach us about the meaning of the cross?

HOW CAN I BE SURE OF MY FAITH?

Icebreakers

Taste and See

Lay out several glasses with different types of coke or colas in them. Alternatively lay out several bowls with different flavoured crisps. Make sure the young people do not see the bottles, cans, or crisp packets. Ask them to sample the cokes and crisps and see if they can identify the different brands or flavours.

Make the point that in order to discover "the real thing" for themselves they actually had to do something.

★ True or False

Read to the group ten statements, three of which sound plausible but are in fact false. Can they tell the difference?

Make the point that we need to be sure of what we believe.

Various "Trust" games

Divide the group in pairs. One person stands behind another person. The person in front tenses his/her body and keeps ramrod straight whilst leaning back and eventually falling back. The person behind them catches them. The question is...do they have enough faith?!

Small Group Questions

♦ If faith is taking a promise from God and daring to believe that it is true, how willing are you to trust God?

♦ Look at the picture of The Pool (page 79). Imagine that the pool represents your relationship or friendship with God, then where would you be in the picture? (e.g. in the changing room? sitting on the edge? sinking? simply bobbing up and down?)

Bible Study

Luke 15: 11 - 24 The Lost Son

It might be worth giving a special explanation about Parables. e.g."This didn't really happen. It is a story Jesus made up to illustrate a point."

♦ Why did the son leave home?

♦ What happened to him when he left home?

♦ What made him decide to go back home?

♦ What did he decide to do?

♦ What does the picture of the father tell us about what God is like?

If this is a familiar passage to the group, get them to read it and then update it in their own words to fit their own culture.

WHY AND HOW SHOULD I READ THE BIBLE?

Icebreakers

★ Assembly Line

Place in the middle of the room something that needs assembling and some instructions on how to do it. It can literally be anything from a small tent to a simple model kit! Give them five minutes to work as a team in assembling it.

Make the point that in order to make sense of the construction, you need the maker's instructions.

�֍ In or out

Many people misquote the Bible. Read out the quotes below. Allow three seconds thinking time, then ask everyone to shout 'in' if they think it is a genuine quote from scripture, or 'out' if they think it is not:

1. In the beginning God created the heavens and the earth - IN (*Genesis 1:1*)

2. God helps those who help themselves - OUT

3. Cleanliness is next to Godliness - OUT

4. You must not steal - IN (*Exodus 20;15*)

5. There is a time for everything - IN (*Ecclesiastes 3:1*)

6. Father forgive them, because they don't know what they are doing IN - (*Luke 23:34*)

7. For what we are about to receive may the Lord make us truly thankful - OUT

8. Money is the root of all evil - OUT ('the love of money' is described as 'a root of all kinds of evil' in *1 Timothy 6:10 NIV*)

9. Hell hath no fury like a woman scorned - OUT (Shakespeare, not Scripture!)

10. Don't judge other people, or you will be judged - IN (Matthew 7:1)

11. Turn or burn - OUT

12. Do all you can to lead to a peaceful life - IN (*1 Thessalonians 4:11*)

13. He who would valiant be, 'gainst all disaster - OUT (popular school hymn written by John Bunyan)

14. Do not be fooled: you can't cheat God - IN (*Galatians 6:7*)

Make the point that lots of people think they know what the Bible says. We need to know what the Bible really says.

Dingbats

Get the group to tackle some of the puzzles from this well known game.

Make the point that although the Bible can seem weird or even nonsensical, it is possible to find meaning and relevant advice from it.

Illustration

Get hold of a letter from No.10 Downing Street or Buckingham Palace (simply write to the Prime Minister or the Queen!) and say that you have a letter from the Prime Minister/the Queen.

Make the point that although the letter contains *their* message it is in fact written by a secretary. So too the Bible. It is God's message but written by various different people.

The Bible in three minutes

Props needed: Watch - pint glass - water in a jug - spoon - bottle of iodine - wooden or cardboard cross with a pouch or container fixed at the bottom, at the back - "hypo" crystals (Hypo and iodine available from any photographic chemist). Make sure that everyone in the room can see this display. *Sodium thiosulphate*

♦ Set an empty glass in front of you for the group to see.

♦ Genesis tells us - "In the beginning was God"...He created the world (*pour water into the glass*). Emphasise the clarity and purity of the water - a pure creation.

♦ By only the 3rd Chapter already going wrong and sin enters the world through man's disobedience (*pour one tablespoon of iodine carefully into the water - it should stay* at *the top*) - this sin is then perpetuated by man and spread through all the earth (*stir the water so that the discolouration spreads all over*). God is still there but His original creation is ruined.

♦ God knew this would happen and through the gospels we see God's plan to cleanse man through Jesus - drawing us back to Him from the separation that sin has caused. *(At this point, put the cross into the water; it should have a quantity of hypo in the container - check with a trial run that it is sufficient - put the cross in carefully to prevent the action taking place just yet).*

♦ Note that the cross itself does not, of itself, make any difference. It requires action on our part - we need to believe. (*Move the cross up and down - the hypo will clear the stain leaving clean water*).

Small Group Questions

It might be worth having a copy of "The Message" by Eugene Bakerson. Read relevant excerpts from it and use this to prompt a discussion on the difference between the *message* that God loves us and the *medium* through which that *message* is conveyed.

♦ What do you think about the Bible? Why?

♦ Imagine you were a bookseller. How would you advertise the Bible so as to sell as many copies as possible?

♦ Do you think the Bible has anything relevant to say to young people today?

Bible Study

Mark 4: 1- 8 & 13-20 The Parable of the Sower

♦ What is the difference between hearing what Jesus says to us and doing something about it? (v 15)

♦ What sort of things do you think Jesus meant by "trouble" and "persecution"? (v 16 & 17)

♦ How do we avoid other things in life distracting us from Jesus? (v 18 & 19)

♦ What does God promise to those who hear the words of Jesus and do something about it? (v 20)

How and Why Do I Pray?

Icebreakers

Charades

This is the popular game where individuals act out well known films, TV programmes, books etc.

Make the point that it is perfectly possible to communicate complicated themes without using words. It is conceivable that God can "speak" to us today.

Back to Back

Get the group to divide into pairs. They should sit back to back. Each person has to take it in turns to describe to their partners a peculiar shape which you have drawn for them on a piece of paper. Alternatively, each person has exactly the same number and type of lego building bricks and one person in each pair has to describe a shape or particular construction to their partner.

Make the point that communication with someone you can't actually see is quite hard work. But it can be very rewarding.

★ Blindfold Game

Blindfold the group and direct them verbally around the house, ensuring that if your instructions are followed closely, both people and property will not be damaged!

Make the point that we have to 'tune in' to God's voice when we become Christians.

Illustration

God is always available to hear us and talk to us. Prayer is like having a mobile phone. We may not *always* be talking to God but we can give him a ring, or receive a call, whenever we have the mobile phone switched on.

Creative Prayer Ideas

"Pass the Prayer":
(for a group that are confident at praying out loud or who know each other well):
Someone starts with an object, such as a ball, and prays whilst holding the ball. They then pass the ball to the next person. This person may then say a short prayer but if they would rather not pray out loud they can simply pass the ball on to the next person. This continues until the ball has gone round the group.

"Posture Prayer":
Encourage the group to pray whilst standing up, kneeling, lying flat on their faces, in an upside down position, curled up in a ball...

"Current Affairs":
Video the news from TV or tape it from the radio. Play this to the group and then invite short prayers relating to the areas covered.

"Spinning Prayers":
Get the group to suggest items for prayer. Write these out on bits of paper and place the paper in a circle. Spin a bottle on its side or a pencil etc. and invite the group to pray for the item that the bottle or pencil points at.

"Shower Prayers":
As you have your shower, at the start of the day, picture Jesus washing away your sin and making you clean as the water runs down your body.

"Breathing Prayers":
Find a quiet place to sit. Spend two minutes breathing deeply. As you breathe in, reflect on all of God's goodness, grace and mercy. As you breathe out, give God all your sin and failure. Then thank God for his great faithfulness to us.

"Arrow Prayers":
Use all the visual aids and creative reminders you can to shoot arrow prayers up to God. These can be prayers of thanks, praise or requests. For example, as you see a beautiful sunset, thank God for his creativity. As you eat a meal, thank God for meeting our needs daily, for healthy bodies etc. Thank God and pray for friends and family as you spend time there etc.

Small Group Discussion

Does God always answer prayer?

Describe a situation where something "gets in the way" when someone prays.

e.g. *wrong motives.*

Alice is a Christian and prays to God quite often. Sadly, she is not very popular in class. She doesn't really have any close friends and no one seems to respect her or compliment her. Alice prays and asks God to give her top marks in all her mock GCSE exams so that the rest of the class will take notice of her and respect her.

Ask the group how they think God might respond to Alice's prayer.

Small Group Questions

♦ Imagine that you had created a universe of your own, which had intelligent beings living in it. How would you look to communicate with the members of your universe?

♦ Do you pray? When and why?

Bible Study

Matthew 6: 5-13 Jesus teaching on prayer

♦ What is the best way to pray according to Jesus?

♦ Look at the prayer that Jesus gives us (v 9-13). What sort of things should we ask God to do for us?

♦ Look at v 14-15. How are we to behave towards other people?

WHO IS THE HOLY SPIRIT?

Icebreakers

Attire

Divide the group into pairs. Ask one from each pair to leave the room. Before they leave, they should look hard at their partners who are staying. While they are out, the others change their appearance in some way. E.g. swap some clothes, take something off, etc. Invite those who left the room to return and to spot any changes. See how long it takes to spot them all, or have a time limit.

Make the point that although we are often interested in external appearances, the Holy Spirit is more concerned with changing us on the inside.

★ Wire a Plug

Test people to see if they can wire a plug properly.

Make the point that for the power supply to come through, we need to be connected properly.

★ Breathing Games

Bad breath game. Give contestants onion, garlic, extra-strong mints, fisherman's friends etc. to eat and get colleagues to smell their breath and guess what it is.

Or have a competition to see if anyone can blow up rubber gloves!

Make the point that The Holy Spirit is described in the Bible as the 'Ruach', the life-giving breath of God.

Illustration

Link in the chain. Hold up a large paper chain. Tear one of the links in the chain and so break the chain itself.

Make the point that often people make a commitment to follow Jesus after many people have influenced them or chatted with them. We are all like links in a chain. Every link is vital for the whole chain to work.

Albert McMakin himself wasn't a great teacher or evangelist but decided one day to invite a friend of his along to a Christian rally. The friend became a Chrstian - his name is Billy Graham and since that time has led thousands, if not millions, of pople to the Lord.

Make the point that only a few people will ever be like Billy Graham; We can all be like Albert McMakin and invite one or two of our friends to hear about Christ. We may never know what enormous effect that tiny action may have.

HOW CAN I RESIST EVIL?

Video clip

"Return of the Jedi" Show the scene where Luke Skywalker fights the Emperor of Darkness.

"Superman III" The scene where Clark Kent fights himself as Superman.

Icebreaker

Root Cause

Hand out newspapers to the groups in pairs/small groups and get them to highlight good news, natural disasters and man made disasters.

Small Group Questions

♦ What immediately comes into your mind when you hear the name, "devil"?

♦ Do you think a power of evil exists?

♦ Do you think it is possible to become *too* obsessed with the occult/evil things?

Bible Study

Ephesians 6:10-20

♦ Look at v 11 - 12.   What kind of supernatural fight do Christians face?

♦ Look at each piece of armour.   What do they represent? How can we acquire each piece?

HOW DOES GOD GUIDE US?

Illustration

Ships and other sea vessels often use two or three fixed points on shore (e.g. a house, a tree and a telegraph pole) in order to ascertain or maintain their exact position.

Make the point that we can often feel "all at sea" but that God provides various ways for us to know where we stand with Him.

Small Group Questions

♦ Do you think God has a plan for your life? In what ways do you think God might reveal that plan to you?

Bible Study

1Peter 1: 3-8

♦ What do you think Peter means by new birth? (v3)

♦ What lies ahead for people who trust in God? (v4)

♦ How can we be sure about the future? (v5)

♦ What should we do when we face difficult problems in life? (v6-7)

WHY AND HOW SHOULD WE TELL OTHERS?

Icebreaker

Light of the World

Give each member of the group a candle. Try and make the room as dark as possible (draw curtains, close blinds, turn off lights etc.). Light a candle and use this to light the candle of the people either side of you. They in turn light their neighbours' candle and so on until the whole group have their candles lit.

Make the point that the whole group can be "lit" simply by everyone "lighting" their neighbour.

Illustration

Which is better? To have £10,000 every day for twenty days or to have £1 which doubles its cumulative value every day for twenty days? (£200,000 compared to £524,288!)

Make the point that we often aim too high, and expect too much too soon, in our attempts to tell others about Jesus. Don't try and evangelise the whole class, or even five friends at once. Better to concentrate our prayer effort on one person and then pray for the process to repeat than try to convert everyone and simply run out of steam.

�֎ Best and Worst

Ask the group to look at the various cartoons (see page 84) and discuss the best and worst ways to tell their friends about Jesus.

Small Group Questions

♦ If you didn't know anything about Christianity, how would you like to be told?

♦ Do your friends know that you come to Church/Youth *Alpha?* What is their reaction?

♦ What are some of the things that put you off telling others?

Bible Study

Acts 8 26-40:

♦ Look at v 26-30. How did Philip respond each time he was told something?

♦ Look at v 34-35. When we tell others about God what subject must we try to stick to?

DOES GOD HEAL TODAY?

Video Clips

A Christian Video with testimony of healing or, better still, have someone come into the group who has been healed.

"Leap of Faith" The scene towards the end of the film where Steve Martin admits he is a fake faith healer because he has seen, in the young boys healing, the real thing.

Icebreaker

Can/Can't Game

This game looks at the difference between things that the group members can and cannot do. Use it to lead into a discussion of God's power and ability to intervene.

Have these challenges written on cards:

♦ Do an owl-hoot by blowing through your hands.

♦ Say six times in fifteen seconds: 'Brave Bob bought a Big Mac and brought it to Barbara'.

♦ Name four countries beginning with the letter 'I'.

♦ Juggle three balls.

♦ Say the alphabet backwards without making a mistake.

Place the cards face down on a table. Ask a group member to pick a card and read it out, but not to do what it says yet. The others in the group have to say whether they think the person with the card can do what is written on it, or not. When all have guessed, the person has a go at the challenge.

Adapt the challenges for your group.

At the end, ask how they made their guesses. How did they guess whether the person could actually do the activity or not? You could get group members to suggest things they think that God can and cannot do. How do they know what God can and cannot do? Can God heal people today? Is there any type of healing he can't do?

Illustration

Fill a small clear plastic bag with water. Cut a small slit or hole in the bag and allow the water to drain out. Point out that the bag did not heal itself!

Make the point that the body is an amazing miracle in itself. God has miraculously placed the ability to heal in our bodies already. We do not leak forever when we accidently cut ourselves.

WHAT ABOUT THE CHURCH?

Video Clips

"Sister Act" An appropriate scene. e.g. the scene where the nuns set up a recreation area for the young people in the community.

"Mr Bean in Church"

"Match of the day" - video any part of the programme where they show all the goals from the rest of the games played that day. Use this to show how grown men and women go totally over-the-top when a man in a thin shrit and shorts kicks a piece of leather into the back of a net. Suggest that for many people a football match is their way of doing church.

Icebreakers

Amazing Facts Quiz

Use the Guinness Book of Records to set quiz questions on amazing human feats.

Make the point that God has made each of us unique and capable of amazing achievement. We are all a vital part of His body, the Church.

Illustration

All tied up. Get between ten and twelve members of the group in a circle. Pass a ball of string around and across the group so that every member is holding on to a piece of string that comes from someone else in the group and goes on to someone else again. There should be a web-like effect created after a while.

Get everyone to hold on tightly and then lean back so that every member of the group is relying on and supported by everyone else in the group.

Make the point that this is how the church should work. You could read out 1 Corinthians 12: 27. As a further illustration, you could cut one of the strands in the web with a pair of scissors. Immediately one or two members of the circle will step or fall backwards. As they do one or two more will also fall away. Eventually everyone will become disintegrated and disperse.

Make the point that the devil loves to destroy the church by breaking the unity amongst its members.

Vox Pop

Use either a tape recorder or video camera to interview various members of the Church. Play the result to the group. Get your group to devise some questions, involve them in the filming or recording.

Get your minister to come to the group and answer any questions they may have about the church, his job etc.

✿ Church Simulation

- ◆ Hide a can of mandarin oranges somewhere near the window. (Out of sight, but not in a difficult place to find).

- ◆ Hide a can opener near the door and a spoon near the light switch. (If different locations are more convenient, adapt the instructions to fit).

- ◆ Write eight role descriptions, as set out below, on eight separate file cards.

♦ Explain that the object of the game is to give the leader a spoonful of his favourite snack! - s/he will need help because her/his hands are tied behind her back!

♦ Each player needs a file card with their instructions - which they should read then put away without showing anyone else.

♦ Encourage your group not to bend the rules by gesturing or muttering.

♦ If there are more than eight players, they take part in pairs or groups which may be of unequal size, the whole group sharing one role. Alternatively, select eight players and ask the others to observe. If there are less then eight, the roles of B and G; C and H; D and E may be combined with only slight adaptation.

A. You are the speaker. You may talk as much as you like, but you may not move.

B. The only words you may use are 'Yes', 'No', 'I know' and 'I don't know'. You may not move. The can of mandarins is hidden near the window.

C. The only words you may use are 'Yes', 'No', 'I know' and 'I don't know'. You may not move. The can opener is hidden near the door.

D. The only words you may use are 'Yes', 'No', 'I don't know' and 'I know'. You may not move. The spoon is hidden near the light switch.

E. The only words you may use are 'Yes', 'No', 'I know' and 'I don't know'. You may move, but only when you are absolutely sure where the can of mandarins, the can opener and the spoon are. You are allowed to touch and carry them, but you must not take them near the leader.

F. The only words you may use are 'Yes', 'No', 'I know' and 'I don't know'. You may only move if you have the can of mandarins in your hand. You are not allowed to touch anything else that contains metal.

G.

The only words you may use are 'Yes', 'No', 'I know' and 'I don't know'. You may only move if you have the can opener in your hand. You are not allowed to touch anything else that contains metal.

H. The only words you may use are 'Yes', 'No', 'I know' and 'I don't know'. You may only move if you have the spoon in your hand. You are not allowed to touch anything else that contains metal.

Set the game in motion and do not interrupt it again unless the participants are struggling so badly that they are giving up hope. The key player is the speaker, so that role should be given to someone who is an imaginative thinker. He or she needs to identify what everyone else may or may not do, and give directions.

When the objective of the game has been achieved, congratulate everyone in the group and give them back their freedom to speak. Invite them to say how they felt about taking part, what their frustrations were, and whether they can think of any way they could have solved the problem quicker. Then ask them whether they have any idea why you asked them to play the game or what you might hope that they will learn.

Small Group Questions

♦ What immediately comes into your mind when you hear the word *Church*?

♦ Has your view of church changed over the past few weeks? If so why?

♦ St Paul described the Church as the Body of Christ (1 Corinthians 12:12-31). If you are a Christian you are part of the body. How does that make you feel? Which part of the body do you most relate to? (e.g. ears - good at listening; eyes - good at seeing ahead, guiding the rest of the body; hands - practical, helper etc.)

Discuss the options for the young people after the Youth *Alpha* course. Youth group membership, discipleship course etc.

HOW CAN I MAKE THE MOST OF THE REST OF MY LIFE?

Icebreaker

Endurance

Ask each group member to choose one activity from a list - for example, staring without blinking, balancing a pen on their nose, juggling singing a favourite tune. Set a timer for five minutes. Explain that they *must* keep going until the alarm sounds, but do not tell them how long it is set for.

Afterwards, get the group members to say how they felt before, during and after their endurance activities. Also ask: 'Did it make a difference not knowing how long you would have to keep going for?'

Make the point that it can be hard to keep going as a Christian. Ask the group how easy they think it is; ask them to be realistic about what makes it difficult and what helps most.

Video Clips

"Dead Poets Society" "Seize the Day".

"Back to the Future" Clips from any of the three 'Back to the Future' films which show how the decisions we make affect our lives in the future.

"Ground Hog Day" Clips to show that each day we are responsible for the right/wrong choices or decisions that we make.